Successfully
Raising
Grandchildren

Successfully Raising Grandchildren

❖

Kevin & Brenda Barnes

Successfully Raising Grandchildren

Cover Design by Atinad Designs.

Copyright 2010
TORCH LEGACY PUBLICATIONS: ATLANTA, GEORGIA;
DALLAS, TEXAS; BROOKLYN, NEW YORK

First Printing, 2010

The Bible quotations in this volume are from the King James Version of the Bible.

The name TORCH LEGACY PUBLICATIONS and its logo are registered as a trademark in the U.S. patent office.

ISBN-10: 0-9830141-0-8
ISBN-13: 978-0-9830141-0-2

Printed in the U.S.A.

To my sisters: Gail Manuel, Catherine Barnes, and Sharon Comery who are all excellent grandmothers.

Contents

INTRODUCTION

———————❖———————

WHILE SITTING AT A LOCAL COFFEE SHOP in Oakland, California, I began to think of how God has richly blessed me with a wonderful family. First, He blessed me with my wife, Brenda. We have been married for over thirty years now. To add to that blessing, the Lord saw fit to place within our care three sons: Kevin, Jr., Keith, and Kenneth. The Lord has doubled our blessing with grandchildren—five thus far. Through our oldest son, Kevin, Jr., God blessed us with three grandchildren: Alejah, Kamani, and Kevin III. Through our second son, Keith, God blessed us with an adorable set of twins: Kyndal and Keith, Jr. Our youngest son, Ken, does not have any children. My wife and I are indeed blessed.

I count it a priviledge and an honor to be a grandparent in a day and time when many grandparents have had to take over the responsibilities of one or more of their children who failed, for whatever reason, to take seriously and to carry out their God-given roles as parents. The Bible tells us in Psalm 127:3-5: *"Lo, children are an heritage of the Lord: and the fruit of the womb is his reward. As arrows are in the hand of a mighty man; so are children of the youth. Happy is the man that hath his quiver full of them: they shall not be ashamed, but they shall speak with the enemies in the gate."*

Too many parents are turning their backs on their children, or are running out on their responsibility to care for their children, and are leaving their children in the care of the state. Of course, many are leaving Grandma and Grandpa to shoulder their parental responsibilities. This should not be. But, be that as it may, being a grandparent is a God-given honor and priviledge.

As a grandparent, the mistakes we made in raising our own children we can help our children not to make in raising our grandchildren. We can, through our years of acquired wisdom, help set our grandchildren on the right path to a successful life in Jesus Christ. If you are a grandparent, I encourage you to enjoy your grandchildren, help train them in the Godly way they should go, and realize you have been, indeed, blessed.

—Kevin D. Barnes Sr.
Oakland, CA

Grandparents make the world...a little softer, a little kinder, a little warmer.
AUTHOR UNKNOWN

CHAPTER ONE

❖

Let Them See Jesus in You

AS A GRANDPARENT, YOUR FIRST RESPONSIBILITY IS to let your grandchildren see the light of Jesus Christ in your life. You can only do that if you have Jesus living in you. That is, over the years you have had a personal relationship with Jesus Christ because at one point in your life you asked Him to forgive you of your sins and to be your Lord and Saviour. If you are thinking, "I can't remember ever doing that. Would you please tell me how I can make Jesus my Lord and Saviour?" I'm glad you asked.

Here is how you can have a genuine and strong relationship with Jesus Christ beginning right now:

1. **You need to understand that you are a sinner.** The Bible says in Romans 3:23: *"For all have sinned and come short of the glory of God."* Everyone in this world has sinned. You are not perfect, neither am I, so therefore, we can never be the perfect grandparents that we may dream of being. Once

we understand that fact, we will be able to humble ourselves and receive God's help in raising or helping to raise our grandchildren.

2. **You need to understand that everyone who dies without Christ will suffer punishment in Hell because of our sins.** The Bible states in Romans 6:23: *"For the wages of sin is death..."* The penalty for our sins is spiritual and physical death in a place called Hell. Hell is a place of separation from God as well as eternal pain and suffering, and God does not want us to have to go through that forever.

3. **You need to understand that only Jesus can save you from your sins.** The Bible says in John 14:6, *"I am the way, the truth, and the life: no man cometh unto the Father, but by me."*

The Bible also says in John 3:16: *"For God so loved the world, that He gave His only begotten Son, that whosoever believeth in him should not perish, but have everlasting life."*

The Bible tells us also in Romans 10:13: *"For whosoever shall call upon the name of the Lord shall be saved."*

If you believe the facts that were laid out above, and are willing to accept Jesus Christ as your Lord and Saviour, please pray the following prayer:

> *Lord Jesus, I realize that I am a sinner in need of a Saviour. I thank You for coming down to earth to die for my sins. I now believe that You are "the Way, the Truth, and the Life." I believe that You died, were buried, and rose by the power of God. I ask You to come into my heart, save my soul and change my life forever. In the name of Jesus Christ I pray. Amen.*

Congratulations on letting the Lord Jesus become the center of your life. Now, with prayer and obedience to His Word, He will give you the wisdom, knowledge, strength and insight to help you raise your grandchildren for His glory.

As you let your grandchildren see Jesus in you, you are introducing them to Jesus in a positive way. Although we live in a great technological age with computers, iPods, iPhones, and other gadgets that as grandparents we may not fully understand, we need to take our grandchildren back to the basics of the Bible. We do that by letting them see Jesus Christ in us.

The history of our grandparents is remembered not with rose petals but in the laughter and tears of their children and their children's children. It is into us that the lives of grandparents have gone. It is in us that their history becomes a future.
CHARLES & ANN MORSE

❖

CHAPTER TWO

Let Them See You Pray

"I exhort therefore, that, first of all, supplications,
prayers, intercessions, and giving of thanks, be made
for all men...that we may lead a quiet and peaceable
life in all godliness and honesty."
1 TIMOTHY 2:1-2

LET YOUR GRANDCHILDREN NOT ONLY SEE YOU pray, but let them hear you specifically pray for them by name. When you do this, you are making God real to them and you are also making them feel special when you call out their name to God. My wife and I not only pray for our grandchildren in private, but we let them see and hear us pray for them.

Oftentimes, while I am praying, my grandchildren will say, "PaPa, what are you doing?" I tell them, "I'm talking to God." They will sit and watch and listen and after I'm finished praying again they would ask, "What are you doing, PaPa?" I will tell them after talking with God, I must take time to listen to God. I can see the wonder and curiosity in their eyes as they try to understand what talking and listening to God really means.

My wife and I not only let our grandchildren see us pray, we take them in our arms and pray with them. We teach them how to pray by letting them repeat after us.

You can begin teaching them to pray by having them put their hands together, close their eyes, and say, "Lord, we thank you for our food. Amen." This is one prayer they will catch on to quickly because oftentimes they are ready to eat. Teaching them to thank God for their food each time they sit to eat is teaching them to see God as the provider of their meals. You are also teaching them to have a grateful heart. They learn not to take these daily blessings for granted. It is easier for grandchildren to be thankful when they see their grandparents being thankful as well.

Do not ever think your grandchildren are too young to learn to pray. They may not be able to verbalize a prayer, but they understand what is going on. So it is important that you be consistent in your prayer life and in teaching them to pray. I cannot emphasize enough the importance of letting them see you have a personal devotional time with the Lord. This is teaching them the importance of meeting with God so that He can guide their life.

As a pastor, my grandchildren witness me praying often, in my quiet time with the Lord, or just randomly praying throughout the day. I do not shoo them away; instead, I invite them to pray with me. I allow them to see how important prayer is in my life and how it can be the same in their lives.

When they have a problem or something is bothering them, teach them to pray about it. When they cannot find their favorite toy, teach them to pray about it. When they express dissatisfaction about something, teach them to pray about it. When they are restless and irritable, teach them to pray.

One thing I want my grandchildren to say about me as they grow older is this: PaPa was a man of prayer. PaPa always talked to God. PaPa talked to God about everything.

Let your grandchildren know that prayer changes things. Let them know that prayer changes people. Let them know that prayer changed you and that prayer can change them too if they will let it. The only way they can know this is by seeing and hearing you pray to God.

Nobody can do for little children what grandparents do. Grandparents sort of sprinkle stardust over the lives of little children.
ALEX HALEY

❖

CHAPTER THREE

Let Them See You Read the Bible

*"Heaven and earth shall pass away:
but my words shall not pass away."*
MARK 13:31

THERE WAS A STORY TOLD ABOUT THIS grandmother who went to church every Sunday. One day she asked the pastor over for dinner and the pastor accepted the invitation. The next Sunday, the pastor went to the grandmother's home and she opened the door and greeted the pastor as she let him in. She told the pastor she had a wonderful granddaughter living with her. As the granddaughter came down the stairs, the grandmother wanting to impress the pastor, said to her granddaughter, "Molly, go upstairs and get the good book—you know the good book; the one you see grandmother read all the time. Go upstairs and get it." The little girl said, "Granny, the good book, the one you read all the time?" The grandmother said, "Yes." The granddaughter came downstairs with a J. C. Penney Spring Catalog and said, "Here, Granny. This is the book I always see you reading."

Our grandchildren need to see us reading more than any other book, the Word of God.

As you let them see you read the Word of God, let them see you obey the Word of God. Talk to them about the blessings that come from obeying the Word of God. Share with them Psalm 119:9 which says: *"Wherewithal shall a young man cleanse his way? By taking heed thereto according to thy word."*

Also share with them Psalm 119:105 which states: *"Thy word is a lamp unto my feet, and a light unto my path."*

As you let them see you read the Bible, let them see you memorize the Word of God. Share with them the importance of doing so by sharing Psalm 119:11 with them: *"Thy word have I hid in mine heart that I might not sin against thee."* Explain to them that the Word of God will guide them to do the right thing and will keep them out of trouble.

As you let them see you read the Bible, let them see you study and meditate on the Word of God. Teach them from a young age to hide God's Word in their hearts. There is a blessing from doing so as it will come to their minds when they need it.

As you let your grandchildren see you read the Bible, teach

them to respect the Word of God. Grandparents, do not use God's name in vain or use God's Word loosely. Also, don't let them see you put anything on the Bible and don't let them put anything on the Bible. This is teaching them disrespect for God's Word. Remember, children oftentimes learn by example rather than by word. Isn't it amazing how you can engage in conversation with someone in the presence of young children and they can repeat almost verbatim anything negative you may have said in that conversation? So speak positively about the Bible and about God.

Buy your grandchildren Bible stories if they are young, and if they are older, buy them Christian classics and other Bible related books. You will never run out of Bible truths to share with them—truths that can be taught over and over again. You help feed their minds and spirits with Godly things and do not leave it up to the world to do so.

Let them see you pray and read the Word of God often because we cannot expect to properly feed our grandchildren's minds and spirits if we do not properly feed our own minds and spirits.

*What children need most are the essentials
that grandparents provide in abundance.
They give unconditional love, kindness,
patience, humor, comfort, lessons in life.
And, most importantly, cookies.*
RUDOLPH GIULIANI

CHAPTER FOUR

Let Them See You Go to Church

"I was glad when they said unto me,
let us go into the house of the Lord."
PSALM 122:1

MY BEING A PASTOR, I GUESS I have an advantage over many of you as far as letting my grandchildren see me go to church. This is important. Teach them from an early age the importance of going to church by letting them see you go to church—and not just on Easter Sunday or on Christmas Sunday, but every Sunday of the year, if possible. This is a great way to teach them about God and to teach them to revere the Word of God as they hear it being preached from the pulpit. This is also a great way to teach them to do ministry for the Lord as they use their talents that God has given to them within the church.

Share with them the blessings of going to church and taking part in church activities. Some of those blessings are as follows:

1. They will be surrounded by people who love the Lord.

2. God will be pleased to see them in His house.

3. They will have the opportunity to meet Godly friends.

I have been extremely blessed to not only have my sons and their wives to attend the church where I pastor, but to also have my grandchildren to attend as well. And just as the Lord gave me insight into my children's musical talents and abilities, which they are using for the Lord, He will give you insight into your grandchildren's talents and abilities so that you can train them to use those talents for the Lord. For example, here are some insights that God has given to me in regards to five of my grandchildren:

Alejah loves to dress and sing. I think she is going to be a Christian fashion model and songstress.

Kevin III is shy and loves to read and write. I think he is going to be a Christian journalist. We buy him Christian books to read and provide him with paper and pens to write.

Kamani loves to talk. She might just be a great Christian

motivational speaker. We converse with her and encourage her to share with us her thoughts and ideas.

Kyndal loves to dance. She will dance on the floor, the table, or wherever—she just loves to dance. I think she is going to be a praise dancer. She may be following in her father's footsteps; that is, having a love for music.

Keith, Jr. is a very active child. He loves to speak into the microphone. I think he is going to be a great Christian preacher (following in his grandPaPa's footsteps. And you guessed it—I love that!)

Grandparents, we can and should help our grandchildren to realize their gifts and potential and help them to realize they can be all God wants them to be. But above all, we need to encourage them to use their talents and abilities for God's glory, and they can begin in the church.

Surely, two of the most satisfying experiences in life must be those of being a grandchild or a grandparent.
DONALD A. NORBERG

CHAPTER FIVE

❖

Let Them See You Respect Their Parents

"Submitting yourselves one to another
in the fear of God."
EPHESIANS 5:21

ONE DAY MY OLDEST SON WAS DISCIPLINING his son. I did not like the way he was doing it, so I jumped in and told my son to leave him (my grandson) alone. I was wrong because Kevin III is not my son; he is my grandson. What I should have done, is pull his father aside in private, and share with him that, in my opinion, he was not disciplining his son in the right way.

As grandparents we sometimes forget how tough we were with our children, and we tend to have a softer heart with our grandchildren. But we must show respect to our grandchildren's parents so as not to cause any animosity or disrespect to develop between the child and their parents, or between you and your children.

What are some areas in which you can show respect for

your grandchildren's parents?

First, you can show respect by not speaking negatively of their parents. You know their faults and failures, but it is not your job to paint a negative picture of their parents in your grandchildren's minds. Ephesians 4:29 says: *"Let no corrupt communication proceed out of your mouth, but that which is good to the use of edifying, that it may minister grace to the hearers."* Encourage your grandchildren by speaking positively of their parents because there is some good in everyone. Any negative thing you feel you have to say, speak directly to the parents in private.

Second, you show respect for the parents by reinforcing the rules the parents set. If your grandchild comes to you and says something to this effect: "Grandma/Grandpa, my mom and dad say such and such but may I please do the opposite?" As a grandparent, your job is to reply: "You do as your parents say." Teach them Ephesians 6:1-3 which states: *"Children, obey your parents in the Lord: for this is right. Honour thy father and mother; which is the first commandment with promise; That it may be well with thee, and thou mayest live long on the earth."* You wanted your children to obey you, so shouldn't you want the same for your grandchildren toward their parents?

Third, you show respect for their parents by not

allowing your grandchildren to talk back to their parents nor to speak ill of their parents no matter how wrong their parents may be. If a child learns to respect his or her parents, he or she can go a long way in life.

My grandson, Kevin III, said to me one day, "PaPa, I don't really want to go to school. I want to stay home. Could you tell my dad?" Of course I could tell his dad to just let him stay home. But his coming to me told me that he and his dad had already discussed that issue or he instinctively knew that his dad would not go for his staying home from school for no apparent reason. So, I took him aside to find out why he did not want to go to school. He told me why and I saw this as a time to listen and to show him that I cared enough for how he felt, but I had to honor his father's wish for him to go to school. So I explained to him the importance of going to school and getting an education and ended with, "Now, go ahead on to school and do your best." After he came home from school, I reinforced what I said to him earlier by telling him how proud PaPa was of him.

Let your grandchildren see you respect their parents by talking respectfully about them, honoring the rules that they set down, and encouraging your grandchildren to do the same.

*Some of the world's best educators
are grandparents.*
CHARLES W. SHEDD

CHAPTER SIX
❖
Talk to Your Grandchildren

"Let your speech be always with grace,
seasoned with salt, that ye may know how
ye ought to answer every man."
COLOSSIANS 4:6

MANY PARENTS ARE CAUGHT UP IN THE rat race of making ends meet that they hardly make time to talk with their children. With the advancement in technology, many use the television, the Internet, the iPod and other devices to "talk" to their children for them. Children still need to be spoken to verbally with love. Our grandchildren need for us to talk with them. Grandparents make use of whatever time you have with them by talking with them and sharing life lessons with them.

Ask them about school. Ask them what they are learning and expand upon it. Let them explain to you some of the new things they are learning that maybe you are not too familiar with. Ask them about their friends.

Talk to them about how things were when you were growing up. They may laugh at how things were different, but they will appreciate the time you took to share with them. When you share your past with them you are helping to shape their future and hopefully make it a better one. Share with them some of the mistakes you made while growing up and some mistakes you made even as an adult so they can avoid making those same mistakes. Life is too short and too precious for future generations to make the same mistakes that former generations made, simply because they did not learn from their parents' and grandparents' mistakes.

Teach them everything you know about your heritage, about your parents and grandparents, and about history and life in general. When you give this knowledge, they will have a better understanding of who they are and of who they can become.

Get in your grandchildren's head. Find out what they are thinking. Sometimes your grandchild will more readily open up to you when he or she finds it hard to open up to their parents. And, in getting into their heads, getting into their world, don't be alarmed at some of the oftentimes surprising things they do or say. Some of the differences in time, culture, and generation will come into play when talking and interacting with our grandchildren. Do not be alarmed at this. The Bible states that all are born sinners—even our precious grandbabies. Each generation ought to get better having learned from the mistakes of the past generation, but sadly, this is not always the case.

I remember one day when Kevin III came into the house and said to me, "Look, PaPa. I got this from my friend at school." It was a toy gun. You may not see anything wrong with a toy gun, but I do. I do not want any of my grandchildren pointing a finger, let alone a toy gun at anyone and pretending to shoot them dead. Horrible things like murder and other atrocities begin in the mind before they become a reality. I told him, "We don't play with guns. Give that toy gun to your father and let him return it to your friend at school."

We must not only protect our grandchildren from the evils of this world, but we must also talk with them about the evils of this world. We must tell them how sinful this world really is and help prepare them for life. Don't let your grandchildren come over and plop themselves down before the television watching whatever is on. You keep the remote control in your hand and monitor what they look at on the screen. Young grandchildren are at an impressionable age and what they see and hear from television, radio, and other means can easily influence their young minds.

Grandparents, we are going to pass off the scene soon, so

let us determine to leave something positive behind for our grandchildren. Even though we may not be with our grandchildren for their entire lives, our words of Godly wisdom can continue to ring in their ears as they go through life and face opportunities to make crucial decisions.

To show a child what has once delighted you, to find the child's delight added to your own, so that there is now a double delight seen in the glow of trust and affection, this is happiness.
J.B. Priestley

CHAPTER SEVEN

Life Lessons to Teach Our Grandchildren

"For the Lord giveth wisdom: out of his mouth
cometh knowledge and understanding.
He layeth up sound wisdom for the righteous:
he is a buckler to them that walk uprightly."
PROVERBS 2:6-7

There are so many life lessons we can impart to our grandchildren for the time that we are with them. Solomon, the wisest man who ever lived, tells us to *"Fear God, and keep his commandments: for this is the whole duty of man"* (Ecclesiastes 12:13). We teach our grandchildren to fear God by instilling in them Biblical principles and teaching them from the Bible.

Below are three life lessons that I believe are very important for our grandchildren to learn from us:

1. **Teach them to respect other people and to respect other people's property.** Often my grandchildren will fight over each other's things.

My granddaughter, Kamani, believes everything belongs to her and no one else. When she wants something she wants it now. She always wants her cousin Kyndal's toys. You ask: How old are they? Kamani is three and a half years old and Kyndal is three years old. You may say, that's too young to try to teach them anything—especially respect. No, it's not. Young children understand far more than we give them credit for. They may not be able to verbalize what we say, but they can understand it. So we have to teach them to share and to respect another person's property and belongings from a young age. By the way, always speak to them in plain English, not baby talk, no matter how young they are.

2. Teach them the importance of hard work and the importance of taking care of what belongs to them. Don't always clean up behind them. After they come to Grandma's house for a visit, don't let them leave without cleaning up. Show them how and where to put up their toys or anything they may have pulled out of place while they are there. Depending on how old they are, let them help wash dishes, vacuum, sweep, and mop. And show them by your good attitude that work can be fun.

3. Teach them the importance of saving. Don't

just give them money to spend. Teach them the importance of giving to God first, and second, the importance of saving some of their money. Teach them to think about how they will be spending their money and to ask themselves, Do I really need this item right now? Or, what would happen if I did not have that thing I want so badly? Share with them instances where you had to save money and how it came in handy when you needed the extra money. Share with them situations when you did not manage your money well and the consequences you reaped for doing so.

Grandparents, the greatest investment you can make in your grandchildren's lives is to instill within them Godly, life-changing values that will be of great benefit to them as they grow older.

*What is it about grandparents that is so lovely?
I'd like to say that grandparents are God's
gifts to children. And if they can but see,
hear and feel what these people have to give,
they can mature at a fast rate.*
BILL COSBY

CHAPTER EIGHT

More Lessons to Teach Your Grandchildren

Hear instruction, and be wise, and refuse it not.
PROVERBS 8:33

TEACH YOUR GRANDCHILDREN NEVER TO BE AFRAID AND that they *"can do all things through Christ who strengthens them"* (Philippians 4:13).

I recall my oldest grandson, Kevin III, did not want to play Tee ball (baseball for little kids). His father asked him if he wanted to, but Kevin III did not want to. I remember pulling him aside and asking him, "Why don't you want to play ball?" He said, "PaPa, I've never played Tee ball before." I shared with him that there is nothing to be afraid of and that there is a first time for everything. I also told him to go ahead and play and that he will enjoy himself. Well, he did and he loved it. In fact, I went to one of his games and Kevin III was strutting around as if to say, "PaPa, I'm going to hit this ball out of the park." Lo, and behold, he got up with all of that confidence and hit the ball out of the park. It was a home run. He looked at me and smiled. "PaPa, I did it!" "You sure did," I said and gave him a big hug.

Teach them to encourage each other. Often times I watch Keith, Jr. and Kyndal. If Keith falls down, Kyndal will always help to pick him up and hug him as if to say, "It's going to be okay. I'm here to encourage you even when you fall." All of us need someone to give us a helping hand and a little encouragement at times. As grandparents, we should teach our grandchildren to encourage others by encouraging them.

Teach your grandchildren to dream big and show them that with God's help they can be anything they want to be. A good example of this principle is our president, Barack Obama. He had a dream as a little child to one day become president of the United States. What made that dream special was that he was a black child and his becoming president would be a first in American history. Well, he kept on dreaming, and I am sure his mother and his grandparents had a lot to do with helping him to keep that dream alive by encouraging him each day and telling him, "You can do it. You can be whatever you want to be. God is there to help you."

Grandparents, just those four words—You can do it—can take your grandchildren a long way. So let's teach them to never be afraid and never to say "I can't," but always "I can."

Below are some wise words from King Solomon that you should take the time to instill in your grandchildren:

1. *"My son, if sinners entice thee, consent thou not"* (Proverbs 1:10). Teach your grandchildren to think for themselves and not to follow others in doing evil.

2. *"My son, hear the instruction of thy father, and forsake not the law of thy mother"* (Proverbs 1:8). Teach your grandchildren to obey their parents and to take heed to their good advice.

3. *"Hear, ye children, the instruction of a father, and attend to know understanding"* (Proverbs 4:1) Teach your grandchildren to pay attention in school and to listen to the good advice of their parents, their elders, and their teachers.

4. *"Keep thy heart with all diligence; for out of it are the issues of life"* (Proverbs 4:23) Teach your grandchildren to keep a pure heart, mind, soul, and spirit.

5. *"The fear of the Lord is to hate evil..."* (Proverbs 8:13). Teach your grandchildren to have a healthy fear (respect) of God and to abstain from doing evil.

Grandparents, remember that what we do and say will influence our grandchildren not only today, but for the rest of their lives. Let's influence them for good.

"Because grandparents are usually free to love and guide and befriend the young without having to take daily responsibility for them, they can often reach out past pride and fear of failure and close the space between generations."
JIMMY CARTER

CHAPTER NINE

Love Your Grandchildren With Tough Love

*For whom the Lord loveth he chasteneth, and scourgeth
every son whom he receiveth.*
HEBREWS 12:6

"GRANDPARENTS ARE SUPPOSED TO SPOIL THEIR GRANDCHILDREN and let them get away with any and everything." That is what I heard many times throughout my life and I never believed it because my grandparents never spoiled me and they never let me get away with anything. My children's grandparents never spoiled them and they never let them get away with anything. And I will not spoil my grandchildren by letting them get away with anything.

That is what I mean by tough love. Even though you love your grandchildren very much, sometimes you have to let them know that their behaviour is unacceptable and will not be tolerated. This type of instruction is love as well. Life does not consist of constantly buying things for our grandchildren and letting them get away with misbehaviour. We must be balanced and love them by training them in the good and Godly way. Sometimes, this is in the form of what Dr. James Dobson called "tough love."

So, how can you show your grandchildren tough love? Here are some principles to follow:

1. **By telling them the truth about themselves.** Solomon tells us that *"Open rebuke is better than secret love"* (Proverbs 27:5). That is tough love. We want our grandchildren to love us and we tend to give in to their desires, but we help them best when we tell them the truth about themselves even if that truth is negative.

2. **By helping them to change their negative mentalities and attitudes.** Sometimes they may not like it when you tell them to change their attitude because they do not feel as though they should. But, you must be lovingly firm with your grandchildren and let them know that having a negative mentality and attitude will not help them throughout their life. People do not want to be around a child or an adult with an attitude problem.

3. **By helping them to see the importance of**

telling the truth about everything. If you know your grandchildren lie often, tell them and encourage them to tell the truth. Ephesians 4:25 says: *"Wherefore putting away lying, speak every man truth with his neighbour: for we are members one of another."* Children need to know that if they continue to lie about situations, nobody will be able to trust them, and that not being trusted is a terrible situation.

4. **By helping them to understand the importance of hard work.** Even though I stated this earlier, it is a very important point. As grandparents, we must not allow our grandchildren to spend all of their time playing or just having fun. You must teach them the importance of hard work and dedication to a task until it is complete. 2 Thessalonians 3:10 says: *"For even when we were with you, this we commanded you, that if any would not work, neither should he eat."*

5. **By helping your grandchildren understand the power of words.** Words can be used for good or bad. Negative words can harm other people; positive words can uplift others. If your grandchildren are bad-mouthing others or hanging around people who bad-mouth others or curse and gossip, explain to them that doing this

does not help them advance in life nor does it encourage other people. Teach them that talking about foolishness or things that are not important are a waste of time and energy. Ephesians 4:29 says: *"Let no corrupt communication proceed out of your mouth, but that which is good to the use of edifying, that it may minister grace to the hearers."*

6. By helping your grandchildren to pick good, wholesome friends. Let your grandchildren know that the friends they choose can impact them for good or bad. In fact, as a responsible grandparent, you should take the time to find out about your grandchildren's friends. Proverbs 1:10 says: *"My son, if sinners entice thee, consent thou not."*

7. By helping your grandchildren to understand that there are consequences for wrong-doing. Teach your grandchildren that everything they do comes with consequences. If they do good, the consequences are positive and can come in the form of rewards, privileges, etc. If they do wrong, then the consequences will be negative and can come in the form of punishment, withdrawal of privileges, etc. Also, explain to your grandchildren that they are not entitled to anything. This is especially important for grandparents who have one or two grandchildren. If you are always spending time with them and giving them things, help them to understand that they cannot do wrong and get away with it. Consequences follow every action.

Don't be afraid of them getting mad at you; they will appreciate it later. And when your words fail, always use the Word of God to help set them straight. Remember, the Bible says that *"The Word of God is quick, and powerful, and sharper than any twoedged sword, piercing even to the dividing asunder of soul and spirit, and of the joints and marrow, and is a discerner of the thoughts and intents of the heart"* (Hebrews 4:12).

"Grandchildren are the dots that connect the lines from generation to generation."
Lois Wyse

CHAPTER TEN

Things We Can Learn from Our Grandchildren

...And a little child shall lead them.
ISAIAH 11:6

SOME GRANDPARENTS HAVE THE NEGATIVE MENTALITY OF "I am done raising my children so you keep them at home and you raise them. Don't drop them over here all the time." This is sometimes said to the chagrin of the parents who only want their children to get to know their grandparents.

My wife, Brenda, owns and operates Barnes Family Day Care which we started eighteen years ago. It is a haven for all five of our grandchildren as well as for other children in the community. The children are cared for in a loving, godly environment. We count it a privilege to open up our home each day to our grandchildren and to other children.

When my wife and I both had secular jobs, my mother-in-law, Mary B. Strange jumped in to help us take care of our own children—her grandchildren. She genuinely loved them and did a fantastic job in watching over them and in helping us train them for the glory of God. Now, we are doing the same for our grandchildren. As we are helping to care for and to train them, we are learning some valuable life lessons in return. What can we learn from our grandchildren?

Patience. Once Kevin III spilled some milk on the table, and he just knew I was going to let him have it. He knew I was not going to let him forget that "spilled milk" incident. But I guess I surprised him by saying, "No problem. We'll get a paper towel and dry it up and we'll get you some more milk." He smiled in unbelief thinking: "I can make a mistake and not get yelled at. Wow!" You see, I can do that as a grandparent, but as a parent? No way. I expect my children to be perfect and not to have accidents like spilled milk. I think as we get older, we exercise more patience having realized how patient God has been with us down through the years. So what's a little spilled milk?

How to Eat Right. There was a time when my wife and I could and would consume just about anything we set our eyes on. But when the grandchildren began to come we began to realize that as they are beginning life we are ending ours. So wanting to spend more years with them, we not only began to watch what we eat, but we do the same for our grandchildren—we limit how much candy they take; we give them fruit instead of candy and fruit juice instead of sodas, etc. I must confess, it took my wife and I awhile before we began to eat healthy. My bad cholesterol was very high and my doctor told me I had to change my diet. With the Lord's help, I did just that. We want our grandchildren to know that their body is the temple of God and that they ought to take care of it. Grandparents we have a responsibility as grandparents to watch what our grandchildren are putting in their bellies.

The Importance of Family. As we help train our grandchildren, we too, learn more the importance of family. We see the silly antics that the young ones do and we smile realizing we were once that way. They come to us with a problem and we realize how important we are to them and them to us. They help remind us of our childhood and its innocency—having not a care or worry. They help bring us back to that state.

As you help to train your grandchildren, understand that God may be trying to teach you something from your experiences with them. Take those lessons to heart and allow them to benefit your life.

Grandparents should play the same role in the family as an elder statesman can in the government of a country. They have the experience and knowledge that comes from surviving a great many years of life's battles and the wisdom, hopefully, to recognise how their grandchildren can benefit from this.
GEOFF DENCH

---❖---

CHAPTER ELEVEN

Parenting Grandparents

Train up a child in the way he should go:
and when he is old, he will not depart from it.
PROVERBS 22:6

JUST IN CASE YOU ARE A GRANDPARENT who has had to take on the parenting role of your grandchildren, for whatever reason, do not let it get you feeling down. God has a special blessing for you. Only a truly loving grandparent can take on the role of parenting for their grandchildren. Be encouraged because now you have years of wisdom and experience behind you that can help in raising your grandchildren.

Below are some additional tips for grandparents who have the full-time job of parenting their grandchildren:

Learn from the mistakes you made in raising your own children. Make a decision not to make those same mistakes again. Even now, you can look at your children's lives and see where you may have gone wrong in raising them. You will then have the ability to not make those same mistakes in raising your grandchildren.

Keep in mind that with each generation there will be some cultural changes. Your grandchildren will most likely not see the world the way you see it. Be open for those changes, and by using God's wisdom, lead, guide and direct your grandchildren to make Godly decisions about life.

Make the extra effort to get to know your grandchildren's friends. In fact, let their friends visit your home. Because you are trying to set your grandchildren on the right path, this does not mean that every parent or grandparent is doing the same. Ask your grandchildren questions about their friends. You know better than they do the dangers of negative influence, and it is your job to protect them from people and from things that will harm them. Some people say experience is the best teacher. That may be true, but why risk your grandchild going through a painful experience when a word to the wise will do if it is taken heed to?

Sometimes you may have an older grandchild who is just rebellious and who refuses to do as you tell him or her to do, and because of your age, you do not have the physical strength to deal with them. In such a case, you may have to turn them over to God for the saving of their soul. Not one prayer offered up to God on behalf of a child goes unheard and God will answer in His time. Never give up hope because "all things are possible with God." You can successfully raise your grandchildren for God's glory.

What a wonderful contribution our grandmothers and grandfathers can make if they will share some of the rich experiences and their testimonies with their children and grandchildren.
VAUGHN J. FEATHERSTONE

CHAPTER TWELVE

The Power of Praying Grandparents

Rejoice evermore. Pray without ceasing. In everything give thanks: for this is the will of God in Christ Jesus concerning you.
I THESSALONIANS 5:16-18

There is tremendous power in prayer. The Lord showed my wife and I along with other family members that He will answer our prayers if we persist in prayer and not give up too soon.

There is a story behind my two youngest grandchildren—Kyndal and Keith, Jr. They were both born pre-maturely. They made it to twenty-four weeks in the womb before the doctor put their mother, Tiffanni, in the hospital on bed rest for their safety. There was a very slim chance that the twins would make it past twenty-four weeks. The doctor asked both their parents, my son, Keith and their mother, what they wanted him to do if the twins made it to twenty-four weeks. It was a difficult choice. Of course, they wanted the doctors to do everything in their power to keep the babies alive.

It so happened that both Kyndal and Keith, Jr. barely made it to the twenty-four weeks before Kyndal broke through her sac. This precipitated an emergency C-Section to save both their lives. Keith had left the hospital, but had to rush back when they called him to let him know what was going on. He did not make it in time for the delivery of his daughter, but he arrived in time for the delivery of his son. Both babies who were now considered micro preemies were whisked away to the Neonatal intensive-care unit (NICU).

Babies with low weight such as Kyndal and Keith, Jr., having special respiratory problems, oftentimes need incubators to provide better temperature support and to isolate them from infection. In their cases, they had closed incubators because they needed special respiratory support including oxygen.

What could a parent or a grandparent do at such a time as this? Pray. And pray we did because their life was hanging on a very thin string. And only God could keep that string from snapping.

Shortly after their birth we were able to visit them in the NICU, but only for brief visits. As my wife and I saw their tiny frail bodies our hearts went up to God. The question of why hung on our lips. We agonized and prayed and cried and cried some more for their health. We just shared our hearts' desire with the Lord which was to see both babies grow to good health. We trusted that God would grant us the desires of our hearts because He said so in His Word in Proverbs 3:4-5: *"Trust in the Lord with all thine heart; and lean not unto thine own understanding. In all thy ways acknowledge Him and he shall direct thy paths."* He also says *"Delight thyself also in the Lord; and he shall give thee the desires of thine heart* (Psalm 37:4). We claimed those verses and others and prayed those verses to God each time we prayed to Him about the health issues of our grandbabies.

Each time we visited our grandbabies in their little incubators we would pray for them, and talk with them telling them who we were and that we loved them and that we were there for them. It was not easy watching their tiny chests barely moving as they struggled with each breath. Sometimes Kyndal would flail around in her incubator. Keith, although more sedate, would sometimes jump being more sensitive to sounds. It was found out that he was suffering from epileptic-type seizures and he was treated with such harsh medications.

It was painful to see them struggling to survive. But we just prayed some more trusting God to bring about healing. There were days when we did not know whether or not they would make it. We would get a call at home or at my office saying, "Pray for the babies. They are fighting for their lives." There were times when we thought we had lost them both. It was reassuring to know that God was there all the time holding their little bodies in His hands.

Day after day, week after week, month after month, we upheld them in prayer before the Lord. We could not see any light at the end of this dark journey. All we had was our faith in God to see us through.

We began to see the light when one day the nurses placed Kyndal in Keith's incubator. She snuggled up to her brother and immediately placed her tiny arms around his tiny chest. That brought tears to my eyes. We saw a change in Keith's breathing after his sister was placed in his incubator. After that, most of the time they were both placed in the same incubator. Slowly but surely they began to get better—Kyndal a little faster than Keith. Kyndal came home first but Keith was to follow not too long after.

As the days, weeks, and months went by, both Kyndal and Keith got better. At almost three years old, they are both catching up in size, speech, and coordination. No one can tell they were preemies. They are so precious to us because we know how they had to struggle for their lives.

I thank God for answered prayers. Grandparents, let me encourage you to pray when you do not feel like it, pray when you feel like it, pray when things are going well and pray when things are not going well. Understand that prayer is powerful and prayer to God can bring you through any situation that you may be facing in helping to raise your grandchildren. Remember that with God's grace, strength, and wisdom, you can succeed in successfully raising grandchildren.

Young people need something stable to hang on to — a culture connection, a sense of their own past, a hope for their own future. Most of all, they need what grandparents can give them...
JAY KESSLER

Resources and Further Encouragement for Grandparents

10 Great Books for Grandparents

1. *God Knows Grandparents Make a Difference: Ways to Share Your Wisdom*, by Priscilla Herbison, Cynthia Tambornino

2. *Chicken Soup for the Grandparent's Soul: Stories to Rekindle the Spirits of Grandparents*, by Jack Canfield

3. *The Power of a Godly Grandparent: Leaving a Spiritual Legacy*, by Stephen Bly, Janet Bly

4. *Essential Grandparent: A Guide to Making a Difference*, by Lillian Carson

5. *Preparing My Heart for Grandparenting: Passing on a Legacy of Faith*, by Milt Harris, Lydia Harris

6. *The Gift of Grandparenting: Building a Meaningful Relationship With Your Grandchildren*, by Eric Wiggin

10 Great Books About Grandparents for Children

1. *What Grandmas Do Best, What Grandpas Do Best,* by Laura Numeroff and Lynn Munsinger

2. *Butterfly Kisses for Grandma and Grandpa,* by Alayne Kay Christian and Joni Stringfield

3. *Hooray for Grandparents Day!* by Nancy Carlson

4. *When Your Grandparent Dies: A Child's Guide to Good Grief,* by Victoria Ryan and R. W. Alley

5. *Grandparents Song,* by Sheila Hamanaka

6. *Grandpas Are For Finding Worms,* by Harriet Ziefert and Jennifer Plecas

7. *The Gifts of Being Grand,* by Marianne Richmond

12 Great Websites for Grandparents

1. www.FocusontheFamily.com
   Provides relevant Christian advice on marriage, parenting and other topics.

2. www.FamilyLife.com
   Offers practical help and advice to strengthen marriages and families through conferences, radio broadcasts and other resources.

3. www.ChristianGrandparenting.net
   The Christian Grandparenting Network

4. www.ChristianityToday.com/holidays/grandparents/
   Christianity Today's Grandparents Day Site

5. www.SuccessfullyRaisingGrandchildren.com
   The Official Website for *Successfully Raising Grandchildren*

6. www.Grandparents.com
   For Grandparents, Parents and Grandchildren

7. www.RaisingYourGrandchildren.com
   Help for Grandparents Raising Grandchildren

8. www.GrandLoving.com
   Making Memories With Your Grandchildren

9. www.GrandMagazine.com
   The Website for Today's Grandparents and the
   Kids who Love Them

10. www.GrandparentingBlog.com
    Advice for Grandparents Raising Grandchildren

11. www.Grandparenting.suite101.com
    Featured Articles on Grandparenting

12. www.MyGrandchild.com
    Where Grandparents and Grandchildren Read
    and Play Together Online

Proud as a Peacock!

❖

"Honey," grandma said sweetly as she took the last sip of coffee her little grandson had made her, "why are there two little army guys in my cup?" "Well, they say on TV, 'The best part of waking up is soldiers in your cup.'" Grandma smiles.

Proverbs says *"Grandparents are proud of their grandchildren"* (Proverbs 17:6, CEV) — proud as peacocks.

After our first grandchild, I couldn't imagine having love left over for another. But after another, and another...I learned that a grandparent's love is limitless.

"The bond between a child and a grandparent is the purest, least psychologically complicated form of human love" (Dr. Arthur Kornhaber). Grandparents can offer an emotional safety net when parents falter, passing on traditions—stories, songs, games, skills, and crafts. And, they often have more time.

Kornhaber found that children close to a grandparent are more emotionally secure and have more positive feelings about older people and the process of aging. Grandparents are grand parents. Grand means having more importance than others; foremost; having higher rank; large and striking in size, scope, extent, or conception; very good; wonderful.

At 46, the average American woman becomes a grandmother. Some become grandparents at 29. Baby boomers are becoming grandparents and step-grandparents, adding to the over 60 million in America today. Many grandparents can now petition for visitation rights. Support groups give legal advice.

Modern mobility means many grandparents learn the techniques of long-distance grandparenting. Others provide regular childcare. In almost a million American homes, grandparents raise their grandchildren. Five million live full-time with grandparents.

Our Past
One gift grandparents can give grandchildren is the past—oral histories of the family. "We used to skate outside on a pond. I had a pony," grandma mused. "Wow," said the little girl, "Wish I'd known you sooner!"

Grandpa Jacob gathered his sons and grandsons around him, blessed them, and said: *"God Almighty appeared to me at Luz in the land of Canaan and blessed me."* Jacob related his relationship with God and his spiritual legacy. His recital was remembered and passed on to a thousand generations (Genesis 48).

Paul told Timothy, *"the genuine faith that is in you...dwelt first in your grandmother Lois and your mother Eunice."* Moses said, *"Teach (my commands) to your children and your grandchildren."*

We can't become Christians by being born into a Christian family, but by making a personal decision to follow Christ. Being raised in a loving Christian environment helps.

Our Presence
Spend time with your grandkids. Make your home user-friendly. Grandparents can instill in grandkids a love for God's Word and His people. Talk to them, tell them stories, and read them Scripture.

Charles Spurgeon's life was molded by his grandfather's stories. You, too, have stories your grandchild would like to hear.

Some grandparents record stories their grandkids listen to at bedtime. Vacations, letters, emails, and phones provide time with grandchildren when they are not near.

Our Provision
Grandparents may help provide clothing, books, toys, or college seed money for their grandchildren. A few extras by a loving grandparent can make a big difference.

Our Prayers
Grandparents can give their grandchildren a legacy of

prayer—praying and claiming Scripture before the throne of grace. Samuel said to the Israelites, *"God forbid that I should sin against heaven by failing to pray for you."*

I pray regularly that God will protect my grandchildren and help them grow up to know Christ. One day my oldest grandchild called to say he'd accepted Jesus into his heart—an answer to my prayers.

We grandparents can pray best for our grandchildren because there's a bit of their parents in each of them. We already know a lot about their parents, so we can pray knowingly.

"A life thoroughly committed to Christ, lived and tested over time, seasoned with experience and humility, is more powerful than most people ever imagine. People who have a heritage of godly grandparents carry this influence in their lives sometimes without recognizing its source" (Jay Kesler).

Or as the Bible puts it, *"Children's children are a crown to the aged"* (Proverbs 17:6). And those peacock-proud people who realize it are the grandest people of all.

This article was excerpted from Dr. David Jeremiah's devotional magazine titled Turning Point. Used with permission.

Dr. David Jeremiah is the founder of Turning Point Radio and Television Ministries and senior pastor of Shadow Mountain Community Church in San Diego, CA.

Godly Grandparenting

❖

The 1970s TV series *The Waltons*, set in Depression-era Virginia, offered America a popular but idealized version of grandparents.

Grandpa and Grandma Walton, played by Will Geer and Ellen Corby, lived in a rambling farmhouse among three generations of their very functional family, where they served as fountains of love, wisdom and humor for their brood of grandchildren.

That was only television. In real life, grandparents usually aren't idyllic sources of unfailing love, wisdom and humor. And most families are to some extent dysfunctional.

One theme from The Waltons remains true, though: Grandparents really do play a big role in shaping their grandchildren's lives, for good or ill.

They always have. Almost 2,000 years ago, Paul attributed his protégé Timothy's faith partly to the example of Timothy's grandmother, Lois.

Given these two facts—that grandparents are imperfect,

and that they help shape their grandchildren's lives— Christian grandparents ought to ask: How can we learn to influence our grandchildren for good?

Three experts, all grandparents themselves, recently addressed that question.

Grandparenting is Getting More Complex

The challenges of grandparenting can be as comparatively minor as a technological gap. Grandparents may find themselves frustrated when they try to talk with a teenager who has an iPod's headphones stuck in her ears, who communicates mainly through text messages or Facebook wall-to-walls.

"Technology available to kids is (so) advanced, it's difficult for many grandparents to keep up with this part of their world," says Steve Bly, 64, of Winchester, Idaho, the co-author with his wife, Janet, of *How to Be a Good Grandparent* and *The Power of a Godly Grandparent.*

But far more troubling social shifts now affect grandparents, too. Increased mobility means they're frequently separated from their grandchildren by hundreds of miles.

Meanwhile, other families have simply disintegrated, creating a contradictory trend: millions of grandparents are raising their grandchildren, without help from the kids' parents. Many of these same grandparents work outside the home as well.

Some 2.4 million U.S. grandparents are responsible for their grandchildren's most basic needs, such as food, clothing and shelter, the U.S. Census Bureau reported in 2006. Of these grandparents, 1.4 million are employed in the workforce.

Whatever their situation, grandparents should consider the following suggestions.

Remember Your Children Are the Real Parents. In Most Cases, Grandparents Still Play a Secondary Role.

"Perhaps one of the biggest mistakes (grandparents make) is the blurring of roles between parent and grandparent, or intruding in the parenting process with their own values and ways of doing things," says Cavin T. Harper, 60, of Colorado Springs, Colo. Harper is the founder of the Christian Grandparenting Network.

A Grandparent Should Try to be a Benign Presence, Not a Toxic One. Don't Offer Advice Unless You're Asked.

Janet Bly, 63, Steve's wife, says grandparents should practice "affirming and encouraging" their adult children, but also try "backing away and releasing the parents in prayer when they disagree with their choices. Meddling can be a big problem."

"Sit down with your adult children and ask them how you can best contribute in a positive and healthy way to their needs and concerns about parenting," Harper suggests. "It is good to talk about boundaries on both sides."

Be Intentional

Grandparents often assume that strong relationships with their grandchildren will develop naturally. That's not always the case. Grandparents must take the initiative.

"One thing's for sure," says Steve Bly, "grandparents must give concentrated time and effort to their relationships with their grandchildren. It won't happen automatically anymore. Some creative means of interaction must be considered."

Don't Play Favorites

Children catch on quickly if a grandparent prefers another grandchild.

"It's important to understand the differences in personality, talents, interests and needs—what each child needs especially from you," Janet Bly says. "The key is for each grandchild to feel that they're loved and treasured, just as they are."

Take Time to Have Fun

Janet Bly remembers a day her granddaughter Miranda, then four, came to visit. Janet was busy with a long "to do" list of her own.

But Miranda wanted to hike to a bridge a mile from Janet and Steve's house. Reluctantly, Janet gave in. Along the way, they stopped to look at what Janet calls "critter prints." They gazed at the lake the bridge spanned. Janet was ready to head home.

As Janet tells it, Miranda said, "'But Grandma, look at all the trails on the other side. I've never been on all those before.'

"Miranda led as she plowed down narrow, winding paths, over boulders, and around fallen timbers," Janet says. "Then she stopped. 'Look, an F-stick!' She picked up a small limb with two horizontal bends. A few steps later she reached for another stick, insisting that it was an 'I.' 'Grandma,' she exclaimed, 'this forest has letters in it. Let's find all the words and make a story!'"

Janet found her own sense of wonder suddenly reawakened.

Moral: The To-do List Can Wait. Take that walk.

Quietly Counteract Our Culture's Negative Influences

Don't overlook opportunities to talk with your grandchildren about your trust in God.

Harper started the Christian Grandparenting Network largely because he wanted to help other grandparents pass on their spiritual insights.

"My personal motivation is my concern about an entire generation growing up neither knowing the Lord nor the amazing things He has done for us," he says.

Let the Bible Teach You

Steve Bly says grandparents should follow Matthew 6:33: *"But seek ye first the kingdom of God, and his righteousness; and all these things shall be added unto you"* (KJV).

"That's the key for any believer," he says, "but especially for grandparents as they hassle with the ... stresses of dealing with the younger generation. Keeping their own faith walk where it needs to be right now, in the midst of what's going on in their present circumstances, is of key importance."

Janet recommends Ephesians 4:32 (NIV): *"Be kind and compassionate to one another, forgiving each other, just as in Christ God forgave you."*

That verse, she says, is good "for any relationships and all the seasons of life and the various kinds of challenges we encounter in them."

Pray

If you're a grandparent, this suggestion is self-explanatory.

Paul Prather is pastor of Bethesda Church near Mount Sterling, KY. He is the author of "A Memory of Firelight." Used with permission.

What All Children Need
From Their Grandparents

If I had to pick one thing that I regret about my childhood, without hesitation, I would choose not having spent more time with my grandparents. Although I did not see my grandparents very often, I do remember that my dad's mother had a great sense of humor. One of my favorite memories of my grandmother was when she read The Three Little Pigs story and then chased us around the house holding her false teeth, screaming: "All the better to eat you with!"

Since the birth of my daughter Taylor, it has been a privilege to watch her interact with my parents. I remember the first time my mother took Taylor out on a special date. When they returned home, my mother proudly informed me that she had taught Taylor how to blow "Raspberries" with her tongue. Having no idea what that meant, I picked her up only to get about three gallons of saliva sprayed in my face. Furthermore, one time I left Taylor with my father so that I could go jogging. When I returned home, I discovered my dad sound asleep in his favorite chair. As I quickly glanced around the room for Taylor, I found her on a blanket with Ralph, my parent's

Siamese cat, sleeping on Taylor's chest. Now I can understand what my parents mean when they joke about getting "even" when I have children!

It's so special to watch a child's face when they are with their grandparents. It's like the excitement kids seem to experience on Christmas morning when they first see the presents under the tree. As a father, I am thrilled that my daughter will have the opportunity to spend time with her grandparents. The best part, however, is watching my parents provide Taylor with a gift that will impact her life forever.

A Priceless Gift Any Grandparent Can Give

An essential aspect of quality grandparenting is realizing that you can provide each grandchild with a very special gift. The gift involves recognizing that the life style you live day in and day out is much more powerful than what you say. The experts are helpful, because they suggest that children learn more from observing what others do, than from what they say. If your desire is to have an impact upon the life of your grandchild, it's helpful to remember that he cannot hear what you say until he observes what you do!

Recently, I came across a poem called "Influence" that illustrates the incredible impact that a grandparent can have on his grandchild:

There are little eyes upon you,
And they're watching night and day;
There are little ears that quickly
Take in every word you say;

There are little hands all eager
To do anything you do;
And a little boy who's dreaming
Of the day he'll be like you.

You're the little fellow's idol;
You're the wisest of the wise;
In his little mind about you,
No suspicions ever rise;

He believes in you devoutly,
Holds that all you say and do,
He will say and do, in your way
When he's a grown-up like you.

There's a wide-eyed little fellow,
Who believes you're always right,
And his ears are always open,
And he watches day and night;

You are setting an example
Every day in all you do,
For the little boy who's waiting
To grow up to be like you.

—Author Unknown

The Diminishing Role of Grandparenting

Children always seem to be searching for the right person to pattern their lives after. Unfortunately, in our society today it feels like the importance of grandparenting is diminishing. Instead of encouraging grandparents to give of themselves, our society promotes athletes, musicians and movie stars as "role models" for our children. Grandparents all across the country have paid a price, and the adversary has won a tragic victory.

As drug abuse, teen pregnancies, and divorce rates continue to rise, now more than ever grandparents need to reclaim their significant role. In doing so, it's important to remember that children do not expect a "superhero"— just you with all your encouragement, affirmation, and love. As I have long regretted the little time spent with my grandparents, I encourage you to become involved in the lives of your grandchildren before all they have left are a few memories.

Likewise, as a society we need to realize the great importance of grandparents. What an honor for any family to have a grandfather who shows his grandson what it means to be a man of integrity, or a grandmother who teaches her granddaughter how to be a Godly woman. It is for these very reasons that the Apostle Paul recognized the importance of modeling when he wrote in Philippians 4:9: *"The things you have learned and received and heard and seen in me, practice these things; and the God of peace shall be with you."*

The Key to Becoming a Role Model

The best way to become a role model is to imagine the type of man or woman you would like your grandchild to become someday. With the image of your grandchild in mind, in what specific ways does your life reflect those same characteristics and values you hope he'll have? Ask yourself: "What does my grandchild observe when he looks at me? Does she see a person who has integrity, honor and wisdom? I encourage you to create a list of the values that you hope will be a part of each child's life. During times that you're together, model those very characteristics so he can begin to, as the Apostle Paul mentioned, *"practice these things."*

For your grandchild, become a person who understands the importance of sharing love with encouragement, affirmation and involvement. The next time you see your grandchild, remember that in fifty years it will not matter what kind of car you drove, what kind of house you lived in, or how much you had in your bank account. What will live on for generations, however, is a simple, but priceless gift—you were important in the life of a child.

Dr. Greg Smalley lives in Siloam Springs, Arkansas with his wife, Erin, and four children. He and his wife work together at the Center for Relationship Enrichment. Used with permission.

The Challenges and Blessings of Raising Grandkids

❖

The Word says, *"Train up a child in the way they should go and when they are old they will not depart from it."* We believe in the word of God wholeheartedly and trust our Lord without question. We also know as the span of time runs through our hands, our children for a season sometimes sway to the ways of the world. We are at this time in our lives where we trust the Almighty without question and lean hard on his word.

At this moment in time, where we have had to lay our daughter at the feet of Jesus, we were also given the divine purpose to train up our six year old grandson, Bradley. We have had him since the age of two. The challenges at the beginning were trial and error, and a lot of praying and tears; as he came from an abusive home life. He had been through and seen more than most adults see in a lifetime, but our God is faithful and not lacking in mercy and healing!

We couldn't attend church for almost a year because his

language was so bad. I left my job as a prayer counselor at a worldwide ministry, to spend the much needed time for his healing and training.

Now, four years later, we marvel at the young arrow that God placed in our hands. We take communion together in our home every night. At first Bradley listened, as we tenderly told him what the sacraments meant and why we did this. We would also pray a short prayer afterwards, and then bedtime. Now, a year later, we still do communion nightly, but our prayer time has become much longer, as our grandson has taken it over. During prayer time the other night, Bradley said, "Bow before the King!" He bowed down, as if to show us how. Oh, the joy that filled our hearts and the awe of such a moment. We felt as if heaven was looking down and kissing us! We were beginning to see the fruit of our faithfulness.

Grandparents, may God bless you as you are faithful to the work that God has placed in your hands! A tender, forgiving and merciful father is He. We have all come from different backgrounds, having good and bad earthly fathers, but we can rest and trust in our Heavenly Father as our guide, model, comforter and friend. The Bible says He is our ever present help in times of trouble. We encourage and bless you, as we travel together down this road of grandparenting our grandchildren, training them up in the ways of the Lord, and pressing toward the high calling!

From ChristianGrandparenting.net. Used with permission.

Poems About Grandparents

---❖---

God's Gift of Grandparents

Grandparents are like honeybees;
They are the very sweetest.
They give you hugs and kisses,
And their stories are the neatest.

The honey they produce
Is more valuable than gold,
For this honey is the lessons
That we lovingly are told.

Grandparents want the best for us
And say we can achieve
Any goal that we have set,
If only we believe.

They help us spread our wings
So when we leave our honeycomb,
We'll make the right decisions
Though we be away from home.

Yes, grandpas are like silver,
And grandmas are a gem,
But better than one hundred diamonds
Are the things I learn from them.

-Alyssa Marie Bentham

Grandparents

Few can bring the warmth
We can find in their embrace,
And little more is needed to bring love.
Than the smile on their face.

They've a supply of precious stories,
Yet they've time to wipe a tear,
Or give us reasons to make us laugh,
They grow more precious through the years.

I believe that God sent us Grandparents
As our legacy from above,
To share the moments of our life,
As extra measures of His love.

-Author Unknown

God's Gift of Angels

She rocks another baby...
hums an age old lullabye
She hopes no one is watching
as with thanks, she starts to cry

Remembering the time
when the babies were her own
And her mother told her gently
too soon they would be grown

Lots of bedtime stories,
skinned knees, and tears to dry
Teddy bears, toy trucks and dolls
and kites up in the sky

First days of school, first loves,
the proms, the wedding days
Sand castles and snowball fights
and teaching them to pray

Now, as she holds her grandchild
and gives thanks unto the Lord
She knows to be a Grandma
is motherhood's reward!

-Author Unknown

When God Created Grandparents

When God created grandparents
the world was truly blessed
with all the special joys
that make a family happiest...

For grandparents know how to do
the things that warm a heart,
They touch our lives with loving care
right from the very start...

They show that they believe in us
and all we're dreaming of...
When God created grandparents,
He blessed our lives with love.

—Author Unknown

Chain of Love

Grandparents bestow upon
their grandchildren
The strength and wisdom that time
And experience have given them.

Grandchildren bless their Grandparents
With a youthful vitality and innocence
That help them stay young at heart forever.

Together they create a chain of love
Linking the past with the future.
The chain may lengthen,
But it will never part....

—Author Unknown

Grandmas and Grandpas

Grandmas and Grandpas are everything nice.
Like presents and candy and raspberry ice.
And chocolate fudge sundaes, with cherries on top.
And popcorn and peanuts and grape soda pop.
In winter or summer, in rain or in sun,
Grandmas and Grandpas are wonderful fun!

—Author Unknown

Grandma's Hugs are Made of Love

Everything my grandma does
is something special made with love.
She take time to add the extra touch
that says, "I love you very much."

She fixes hurts with a kiss and smile
and tells good stories grandma-style.
It's warm and cozy on her lap
for secret telling or a nap.

And when I say my prayer at night,
I ask God to bless and hold her tight.
Cause when it comes to giving hugs
my grandma's arms are filled with love!

—Author Unknown

Write Down Your Grandchildren's Names and Ways that You Can Be a Blessing to Them

❖

_____

_____

_____

_____

_____

_____

_____

_____

_____

_____

For More Information About
Dr. Kevin D. Barnes's Ministry and
his Wife, Brenda Barnes, Visit:

www.AbyssinianMBC.org
www.DrKevinDBarnesSr.com
www.SuccessfullyRaisingYoungBlackMen.com

Made in the USA
Charleston, SC
13 October 2010